BOOKED

A STRONG START FOR
YOUR CHILD ACTOR

**By Gloria Iatridis
and Olivia Kate Iatridis**

FriesenPress

One Printers Way
Altona, MB R0G 0B0
Canada

www.friesenpress.com

Copyright © 2024 by Gloria Iatridis and Olivia Kate Iatridis
First Edition — 2024

All rights reserved.

No part of this publication may be reproduced in any form, or by any means, electronic or mechanical, including photocopying, recording, or any information browsing, storage, or retrieval system, without permission in writing from FriesenPress.

Author Gloria Iatridis is also known by her Inuit name of Kinnukana.

Example Headshots: Whitesell Photography

Spotlight artwork: Vecteezy.com

ISBN
978-1-03-919538-7 (Hardcover)
978-1-03-919537-0 (Paperback)
978-1-03-919539-4 (eBook)

1. PERFORMING ARTS, ACTING & AUDITIONING

Distributed to the trade by The Ingram Book Company

I dedicate this book to all parents who love their children; believe in them and support their dreams.

Quyanainni – Thank you!

Kinnukana

Contents

Preface 1
1. Should Your Child Be an Actor? 3
2. Olivia's Acting Pursuit 5
3. Olivia Kate Iatridis 9
4. Mom-a-ger 13
5. The Suicide Scene 17
6. Actor Preparation 21
7. Example of a Resume and Headshots 25
8. Finding an Agent 29
9. Submitting to Casting Directors Yourself 33
10. The Mendacious Agent 35
11. The Great Agent 39
12. Training and Experience 41
13. Mental Preparation and Confidence Building 43
14. Diversity, Inclusion, and Indigenous Representation . . 45
15. Casting Calls 47
16. People Who Think They Are Important and Famous . . 51
17. The Perfect Casting Call 55
18. Auditions 59
19. The Adult Film Producer 61
20. Self-Tapes 65
21. Fun at the Park 67

22. The Script, or Sides....................................69
23. Callbacks...73
24. No Response..75
25. Landing a Role.....................................79
26. It Is Okay to Say No...............................83
27. Olivia's First Callback............................85
28. The Contract.......................................87
29. Preparations Before Filming.......................91
30. Filming..93
31. Different Types of Films..........................97
32. Olivia's First Commercial........................101
33. Knowing Your Own Worth...........................103
34. Big Roles...107
35. Typecasting......................................111
36. Demo Reels.......................................113
37. Pay..115
38. Promotion..119
39. Celebrate..123
40. On Her Own......................................125

Glossary...127

About the Actor......................................133

About the Author.....................................135

Preface

I am not an actor and have not worked in the film industry. But when my daughter told me that she wanted to be an actor, I decided to learn as much as I could to help her reach her goals.

My daughter started acting at the age of thirteen, and as of writing, I have spent the last eight years supporting her as she pursues a variety of opportunities in the industry. She has achieved much success, especially given our family's unique background.

I have been contacted many times by others to share my knowledge about how I encouraged my daughter to be involved in acting. I have also seen many questions on social media from parents who do not know what to do when their child is interested in acting.

There does not seem to be many resources that lay out all the basic knowledge parents need to properly guide their child actors in one book. There are many unwritten rules that drive the film industry, and many parents and new actors only learn them through experience. Sometimes that is when mistakes happen that could impact your child.

I decided to write this book to share my knowledge with others. It is based mainly on my daughter's and my actual experiences over the first eight years of her acting career. I share advice and stories of actual events that will provide guidance for you and your child actor, who may be just starting out in the film industry.

I hope that you enjoy this book, and that it also prepares you to support your child as they pursue acting.

It is not an easy profession, let alone for a child, so if you plan to expose your child to this type of work, learn as much as you can and become knowledgeable of the film industry. It will be key to your child's success. This should also be a fun time for both of you, so do not be too serious!

CHAPTER 1

Should Your Child Be an Actor?

How can you tell if your child should be an actor? It is not a typical thing that all children participate in regularly, like sports or other hobbies.

There are a few signs that your child is showing a genuine interest in acting. Children who have a natural talent for performing around the house to real or imaginary audiences may be great at acting. Children who love movies and talk about starring in them is a sign that they are interested; another sign is when there is a play at school, and they are the first to volunteer or audition for a big part. Children who shine on stage or in front of a classroom may excel in acting.

Children in these circumstances may have a passion for acting, but it is not the only thing they will need in order to be a professional actor.

It is a huge responsibility to be a child actor. A child must be well-behaved and act professionally on set along with other adults and child actors. A child must be able to manage both working and school. If a child often works on set, they must be able to stay on top of homework.

There is no set age to start your child in acting. There are many casting opportunities depending on how old a child is and where you live.

CHAPTER 2

Olivia's Acting Pursuit

I will never forget when I realized that Olivia was her own strong individual person. She was about two years old, and I remember looking at her and thinking, *I have no control over this beautiful little girl.* She had such a strong personality and spoke with such passion about everything.

From an early age, Olivia was always artistic. She would be creating things around the house. She would design her own Barbie clothes and create fashion magazines. She also liked to write her own storybooks.

Whenever I cooked meals, she would be with me in the kitchen, voicing her own commercials about all the ingredients that I was using. She even called commercial breaks. Sometimes she would act like we were on a cooking show and explain to a pretend audience how to make meals.

Olivia would write messages to me and slip her little notes in envelopes under my bedroom door. Olivia always questioned things and was a strong advocate for anything she was passionate about. I used to think that she should be on television because I could sit and watch her all day.

Olivia was always performing, whether she was at home, school, or at her extracurricular activities. When she was little, at age four, Olivia started ballet and dance lessons. Once she turned seven, she took an interest in figure skating. These activities provided an opportunity for Olivia to perform in front of live audiences.

Olivia placed first in all levels of her interpretive skating competitions. The interpretive competitions focused on skaters' creativity, expression, musicality, movement, and interpretation of music. When Olivia was alone on the ice performing in front of an audience, she completely shined.

While at school, Olivia signed up to be part of the school choir. Olivia also tried out for school plays. When Olivia was ten years old, she had the opportunity to audition and was cast in her school play. She landed the role of the Cricket in *Pinocchio*.

Leading up to the play, we had travelled to Florida on spring break for vacation. While there, Olivia practised her lines and prepared for her role. I noticed that memorizing her lines came easily for her, so much so that she managed to learn the lines of most of the characters in the play. When we returned home and Olivia went to rehearsals, she was able to stand in for other characters who were not able to attend.

We were so impressed opening night to see Olivia on stage. She absolutely stole the show. I could not have been prouder of her.

In some ways, I wished I was able to get her into acting earlier, but we lived in the Northwest Territories, Canada, and there were few opportunities there at the time. It wasn't until we moved to St. Albert, Alberta that Olivia was able to focus more on pursuing acting as a career.

One night, I was listening to the radio while sewing, and I heard the announcer speak about an opportunity for children to audition for a talent event. After asking Olivia if she was interested, I immediately picked up the phone and booked an appointment for her.

Olivia and I went to the talent event together, and she went through the audition process. It involved a short interview and having to record a few lines into a camera. Afterward, we were told to wait at home and to be available for a call-back the next day. I knew that Olivia would be called back. She was so confident in her abilities, and the lady who spoke to her drew a star on the top of her application.

The phone rang the next day, and Olivia and I screamed with excitement. She went back that evening with me and her dad and had another audition, but this time it was in front of a director.

It was intense, and we had to wait to see if Olivia would be accepted. Olivia's number was called, and we were so excited that she was accepted to the talent event in Florida. She was assigned a mentor and given assignments to prepare for the event. She prepped for close to a year. Once we were there, she excelled in all the showcases, which consisted of dancing, acting, and modelling. This was the first time she had ever participated in a talent event, let alone an international competition; she won the event's Facebook photo contest and placed in the top ten out of hundreds of children from around the world. She did this in Disneyworld at Orlando, Florida, with no fear. Once again, we were so proud of her.

We were sitting on the plane travelling home from that week-long talent event when I realized that my girl was serious about being an actor. She was thirteen years old at the time. She told me that once she turned eighteen, she would be moving to Hollywood to pursue acting.

I remember staring out the window into the clouds and thinking that I needed to do something to prepare her. It scared me to think that she would run off at eighteen-years-old to pursue something that might not always be secure or safe. But when I saw the look on her face and heard the passion in her voice, I knew I wanted to support her. I also knew, after she participated in this week-long talent event, that this was where she would shine so confidently performing for others.

As I flew through the sky on the plane, I thought about all these wonderful times. I came to the realization that I needed to learn as much as I could about the acting world so that I could make sure Olivia was protected and ready for the industry, especially when she went off on her own.

CHAPTER 3
Olivia Kate Iatridis

Once we arrived at home, we began talking about what Olivia's acting name would be. People aspiring to become movie stars often change their names. Most times, it is done to make the name easier to say or more memorable. With Olivia, I did not want her to lose her identity. As an Indigenous person, knowing who you are and where you come from is important.

Olivia Catherine Seleona Iatridis was born in December 2001 in Yellowknife, Northwest Territories, at 7:30 a.m. She was due on December 12th but decided to enter the world late. She also decided to arrive during a shift change at the hospital and was fortunate to have four nurses and the doctor in the room at the time. She entered the world with an audience.

I originally wanted to name her Olympia so that she had a Greek name like her dad Pericles, but he did not want to name her that. A friend of mine said, "Why not name her Olivia instead?" Her dad and I liked the name Olivia, so we decided on it. It just felt right.

Olivia was given two special middle names—Catherine and Seleona. She was named Catherine after a very special friend of mine, Catherine Mitchell, a Gwich'in Elder. Catherine was a kind and loving person who always welcomed me into her home and guided me as a young adult. I loved her dearly.

Olivia was also given an Inuvialuit name as part of our Inuit cultural traditions. Olivia is Inuvialuk (Western Arctic Inuk) from Canada's Western Arctic. She is a proud member of the Inuvialuit Settlement Region. It is our tradition for Elders to pass on names to children when they are born. My mother, Sarah Anderson, was the one who decided on my girl's Inuvialuit name. She named her Seleona after a wise Elder with the same Inuvialuit name, but also went by the English name of Mary Avik. Mary was from my home community of Tuktoyaktuk, and she was also known as a medicine woman.

We believe in our Inuvialuit culture that children take on the traits of the people they have been named after. I knew that Olivia would have a strong and giving soul the day she received her names.

Olivia wanted to keep her first name and find a shorter version for a second name to use as her stage name. We played around with different names until we decided on Olivia Kate. Kate would be short for Catherine, and both names were easy to remember and spell. I was optimistic about the name until I googled it and realized that Olivia Kate was the name of an apparently well-known adult video star on the internet.

We decided not to use the same name and added in her last name—Olivia Kate Iatridis.

Olivia Kate Iatridis, actress. This is where it all began.

CHAPTER 4
Mom-a-ger

The work began for me too, as a mom-a-ger, a cross between "mom" and "manager." This is not an easy job to take on, and it was important for me to understand my role early on, as I did not want to become a detriment to Olivia's acting career.

First and foremost, your child must be the one who wants to do this. Your role is to put in place the structure that will support your child. This means you may have to do things on a moment's notice, work late at night to help your child with an audition, or spend hours on a set while your child works. At minimum, it is like having an additional part-time job.

As a mom-/dad-/parent-a-ger, you are managing your child's acting career. You are the one arranging for headshots, drafting resumes, registering your child for training, finding an agent, selecting the right wardrobe, filming and editing self-tapes, driving your child to auditions, networking with others, and promoting your child. Sometimes you are even the security guard, making sure your child is safe.

Official talent managers can charge a 15 percent commission of your child's earnings, but some mom-/dad-/parent-agers, like me, do this work for free. I consider it as an investment in my child's acting career.

Being a parent who manages your child's career is hard at times because you are more emotionally invested. There may be times where you are torn about how to handle a situation. Remember that you are a parent first and a manager second.

I have learned so much about the film industry and have gained different skills for my everyday work and life. It is a whole other world that can lead to other opportunities for yourself in the future if you so choose.

Sometimes I do not know how I did everything while also having a full-time job. It was all new and exciting for me too, so I was able to invest my free time outside of my regular job to focus on this role. It did not seem like work for me, and it allowed me to spend dedicated time with my daughter.

It is important that you enjoy what you are doing. If it becomes more like work or just another job, I recommend that you hire someone else to be your child's manager.

I was fortunate that I enjoyed being a mom-a-ger and that Olivia and I had so much fun participating in numerous activities. It also gave me an opportunity to connect on a deeper level with my girl, especially through some of her most vulnerable teen years. We were able to have conversations about important topics that we probably would not have had if she were not involved in acting.

CHAPTER 5

The Suicide Scene

TRIGGER WARNING: mentions of human trafficking and simulated suicide.

In April 2017 I submitted Olivia's resume for a casting call for a docudrama. We received a response with a request for Olivia to attend the audition in person.

At the time, I asked if there were any sides (another word for the script in the industry) that Olivia needed to read in advance so that she could prepare for the audition. The casting director said that sides were not being sent in advance so actors would not form opinions on the character; this would be a cold reading. A cold reading is when an actor does not receive a script in advance of an audition. Instead, they will be given lines at the audition to say without any earlier practise. The director wanted to see how well people did with direction.

Thinking nothing of it, I drove Olivia to the audition. Once there, she went inside the building while I waited in the car. After a few minutes went by, I received a text from Olivia. She said that the casting director wanted to talk to me. I went inside the building and entered the room they were using for auditions. My daughter was standing in front of the room, and there were three people sitting behind a table.

Once I entered, the casting director asked me if I was Olivia's mother. I said yes. They asked me if I had read the information about the docudrama that they were going to film. I said no as I had not received any sides or background information in advance. They told me that the film was about human trafficking and that it would be rated "mature," then asked how old Olivia was. I told them she was just sixteen years old.

They told me she had the perfect look for the role but was too young to be in the film. We ended up having a conversation about human trafficking and the fact that unfortunately, it was young girls like Olivia who ended up in the situations depicted by the docudrama.

I apologized for wasting their time. We wished them all the best with their film and left the building.

A few weeks later, I received an email from the casting director stating that Olivia was selected for a role in the film. I emailed him and asked for clarification, as she did not complete the audition. He told me that they were going to give

THE SUICIDE SCENE

her an age-appropriate role in the film and that parents of minors must be on set while filming.

Later that month, the short film was shot all within one day. My girl worked for thirteen hours straight with only a few short breaks and one hour for lunch. We were told in advance that she would not have any lines to read. However, she was given some as the film was being shot.

Closer to the end of the day, Olivia came outside where I was waiting off set and pulled me aside with concern on her face. She said that the director had selected her among the actors to act out a scene. In it, there was a young girl who was being trafficked, and she ended up pregnant. In the film, the girl was so devastated that she went into the bathroom and committed suicide by slicing her wrists.

Olivia was nervous about having to depict this scene. We went into the house and down to the basement furnace room to discuss it privately. It had already been a long day, and Olivia was tired.

There was a lot of pressure to make this decision right away, with no time to prepare her in advance. We talked about her fears and concluded that this was an opportunity for her to play a stronger role in the film. Although Olivia was apprehensive, she decided she would do this additional part.

Looking back now, as a mom-a-ger, I would have done things differently. First, I would have insisted on more information on this film before even sending her in for an audition. Second, I would have insisted on seeing a script in advance of filming. Also, I would not have agreed with

Olivia working so long on set, especially in the environment they were in. There were a few people smoking cigarettes in the house for the scene during filming. I certainly would have questioned the late addition to her role and insisted that she not do the role given that she was expressing discomfort with the situation.

As a mom-/dad-/parent-a-ger, you want your child to be successful, so there is a part of you that will, at times, push your child to do things they might not want to do. However, it is imperative that you are a parent first; supporting your child to make their own decisions based on their comfort level is critical and should take precedence.

Olivia completed her job on this film, and we had great discussions about human trafficking and the devastation of suicide. It was an opportunity for Olivia to learn more and become an advocate for change.

Many actors use their fame to speak out about matters of importance and to influence others in a positive way. This role gave Olivia and me an opportunity to discuss what platforms she might want to support in the future as a public figure.

CHAPTER 6
Actor Preparation

Many people think it is easy to be an actor. If you have that special look, that is all you need. This is not true. It takes a lot of preparation and training to be an actor. There are several basic things that all actors must have.

Headshots

All actors require professional headshots. For child actors, these should be updated regularly (every six months to a year to the age of eighteen), especially if your child is growing and changing quickly. A headshot is a photo taken from the shoulders upward. It is designed to give a good perspective of what a person really looks like. Headshots should be done in colour.

Your child's headshot is extremely important because you give it to agents and managers when looking for representation. You also submit the headshot when you are responding to casting calls, and you bring it to every audition. It is what casting directors will use to decide whether they want to see your child.

In order to get ready for headshots, your child should have clean and tidy hair and a natural look. It is important to wear plain, solid-coloured clothing with no writing. Your child should wear colours that complement their skin, hair, and eye colour. Make sure your child brushes their teeth and does not wear any jewelry.

It is best to find a photographer that specializes in headshots because general photographers may sometimes modify your photos to the point that your child will not look like themselves anymore. At most, they should only be fixing the lighting or temporary imperfections on your child's face (e.g., fly-away hair or pimples).

Most photographers will give you two sets of photos: web-resolution and high-resolution images. It is important to have both, so they are sized for accurate display on monitors, tablets, and phones.

Make sure you get a variety of shots, expressions, and poses in your headshots: some close, some far, some smiling, some not smiling.

It is important to keep your child's headshots current, and this does take time to manage on an ongoing basis. If you can hire someone to do this for your child, it would be ideal.

Resume

Actors must also have an up-to-date resume to submit with their headshots. An actor resume uses a different format than a work resume and focuses on an actor who is seeking a role in film, TV, or other acting jobs. Most resumes are written to fit on a single eight-by-ten-inch sheet of paper.

The resume should highlight the actor's past acting roles, experiences, and training, as well as their agent and contact information. The resume should emphasize the actor's unique traits, skills, and awards.

Like headshots, you must keep your child's resume current. A great agent will help your child write their resume.

Online Acting Platforms

Agents will also ask actors to sign up for certain online acting platforms. Olivia has accounts on the websites Actors Access, Casting Networks, and Casting Workbook. These platforms function like a virtual database between casting directors and aspiring actors, and they allow actors to maintain profiles and connect with their agents. These online platforms charge a subscription fee.

Olivia's Key Tips for Your Child Actor:

In your headshots, show personality. If you have done modelling photography or currently model and are branching out into acting, understand that your acting headshots are going to be very different then your modelling ones. A good photographer will coach you through poses and expressions, especially if it is your first time, but I suggest going into your session with some ideas about what kinds of characters you are interested in playing. Plan your wardrobe around them and spend some time in front of the mirror deciding what facial expressions you should express for the characters you have in mind.

This style of photo can feel really intimate, so it is best to just commit and test out some of your acting chops. And most importantly, have fun with them!

CHAPTER 7

Example of a Resume and Headshots

Olivia's Key Tips for Your Child Actor:
Put every skill you have on your resume, even ones that might sound silly. They are all important to know. For example: riding a bike, swimming (you do not have to be a trained swimmer, basic, everyday swimming ability is fine), drawing/painting, horseback riding, skating, etc. List everything you have experience with. You never know what skill will be required for filming, and it is helpful to highlight activities that may get you noticed.

BOOKED

Example Only Resume

Olivia Kate Iatridis Height/Weight/Eyes/Hair
Name of Agent

FILM/TELEVISION

Sweeter Than Chocolate (MOW)	Principal	David Weaver / Hallmark
Alaska Daily	Principal	Patricia Riggen /20th TV/ABC
*Abducted**	Lead	Daniel Foreman
Indra's Awakening	Supporting	Kellen Frost

*Nominated for Outstanding Performance by an Actress in a Leading Role, RNIFF 2021

THEATRE

Two Words for Snow	Lead	Richards Sanger

COMMERCIALS

Mattress Mattress	Principal	Planit Sound

AWARDS - selected

Joey Award, Outstanding Indigenous Performer Award, 2022
Joey Award, Best Actress in a Commercial 12–17 Years, 2020
Joey Award, Best Principal or Supporting Actress in a Short Film Age 15–16, 2018

TRAINING

On Camera Fundamentals, Marc Gaudet, Feb – Mar 2021 / ActorVan Studios

SPECIAL SKILLS

Dance: Ballet (10 Years), Jazz & Lyrical (6 Years)
Sports: Figure Skating (7 Years), Swimming, Biking

EXAMPLE OF A RESUME AND HEADSHOTS

Example Headshots

BOOKED

CHAPTER 8
Finding an Agent

If your child wants to be a professional actor, it is necessary to find an agent. There are various kinds of agents throughout the film industry. Different agents cater to different areas of the business, so researching for the right fit is essential. For example, some agents focus on background performers, stand-ins (extras), or stunt doubles for film; some focus on commercials. A good agent can be the difference between moderate and outstanding success.

An agent submits your child's information to a producer or casting director so your child can get an audition. In most cases, it is unlikely your child will get an audition with a casting director without their resume and headshots being submitted by an agent. Additionally, the agent will pitch the actor for roles, follow up on submissions and auditions, and negotiate or renegotiate pay and contracts. Some are highly selective, representing only a few clients, while others maintain a larger client roster.

Agents work for talent agencies that are licensed by the area where they are located (e.g., province or territory here in Canada). This licence gives them the legal right to seek employment for their clients and negotiate contracts.

A good agent is one that is sincerely invested in your child's career as an actor. It is important that you connect with your child's agent regularly to ensure they believe in and are supportive of your child and acting in their best interest.

Agents work on commission and receive 10 to 15 percent of the income earned by the actors they represent. Therefore, the more your child works, the more the agent gets paid.

To find an agent, research agencies and review agent profiles, then put together a list of potential options. Talk to other parents that may already have children working in the film industry. Make sure that you are submitting to agencies that represent the type of work your child wants to focus on. Check to see if the agencies are licenced in your area and read reviews before making any decisions.

Once you have decided on a potential agent, you will need to send your child's resume and headshot, along with a cover letter stating that you are seeking representation for your child. Keep your cover letter simple and clear. Getting a referral to an agent from a reputable acting teacher, casting director, or fellow actor will help with getting noticed, but it is not necessary.

If your child does not have any experience and you do not know what to put in their resume, focus on what current information you have regarding education, volunteer or work experience, extracurricular activities, and any skills that your child may have.

Olivia's resume looked very different at the beginning before she had completed actual acting jobs. As she gained work experience, we adjusted her resume.

Olivia's Key Tips for Your Child Actor:
Review all your contracts carefully. Even though most agents will become your power of attorney (able to sign contracts on your behalf) you should always read your contract before giving your agent the okay to sign.

Speak up if you see something you disagree with, or if something important to you has been left out. You and your agent might have different views on what you require, and your needs might not be met if you do not double-check.

CHAPTER 9

Submitting to Casting Directors Yourself

In addition to the work Olivia's agent submitted her for, I also sought out as many opportunities as possible for her. I did not wait to hear from her agent, and being proactive enhanced her career.

I did several things regularly to find additional jobs for Olivia. I went to her online acting platforms and checked breakdowns to see if there were any that matched Olivia's skills and characteristics. Breakdowns are postings that contain important information about a film and the roles being cast.

I joined several acting pages on Facebook. Searching for pages tied to your location is a great way to find local jobs. Sometimes for small, low-budget films, casting directors will promote through social media instead of other online platforms.

It is important to keep your child's agent informed if you have submitted for a role directly. If your child is invited for an audition, it is good to let your child's agent know right away and have them review the part. Your child's agent can give you advice on whether it is a good idea for your child to participate.

Sometimes your agent may not want your child to participate in a role, especially if certain situations are unknown, such as the dates and times are not clearly stated, the details of the shoot are unclear, or if there is no compensation for doing the work.

CHAPTER 10
The Mendacious Agent

In January 2016, on social media, I saw a casting call for teenagers to be in a feature film. I emailed the director and received a response saying they were interested in having Olivia audition and would be sending further information soon. Olivia ended up auditioning the second week of February.

Out of curiosity, I sent an email to Olivia's agent to ask them if they submitted Olivia's resume for the role, too. They replied to me that they did, but that the director was looking for older actors. I thought that was an odd comment given that Olivia had already auditioned.

I received an email later in February from the director saying that Olivia made it to the top five for a lead role from more than one hundred actors who applied. They decided to give the role to another girl. However, they were so impressed with Olivia that they offered her the role of a waitress and even added in a line so she could have it for her acting reel. Olivia agreed to the role.

Soon after, we received the call sheet. The call sheet lists all the actors and their agents and outlines the schedule and where they need to be for the following shoot day. I noticed that several of the actors cast in the film had the same agent as Olivia. I was so disheartened that the agent was not truthful with me. I knew they did not submit Olivia at all and was not truthful to me about it. If they had, the director would have dealt with them and not me.

I knew we could not work with that agent anymore. They had broken our trust. Honesty is important to me, especially since a child is involved. In March 2016 I cancelled the agent contract and removed that agent from all of Olivia's online platforms. Since the contract said we had to send a formal letter of notification to cancel the contract, I wrote a letter and sent it by registered mail.

Make sure you have an out clause in any contract you sign with an agent that allows you to cancel the contract if needed. If the agent refuses to have an out clause, then I would not recommend using them for representation.

This also happened with another agent of Olivia's. Once again, I submitted Olivia's resume for a casting call for a lead role in a feature film. Olivia received an audition for the lead role. Before I had a chance to update her agent on the opportunity, they sent Olivia an email saying she had an audition for the same film but for a smaller role. There was no mention of the lead role she was invited to.

The agent had not submitted her for the lead role, only a supporting one. Fortunately, Olivia auditioned for the lead role and was chosen for the film.

In both these instances, Olivia's agents had the ability to submit her for lead roles and did not. However, they did submit other people from their rosters. If I had not submitted her resume myself, she would not have had these opportunities.

It is important to make sure your child's agent is held accountable for their actions. They have a lot of control over what jobs your child is submitted for and can in turn have an impact on the success of their acting career.

Olivia's Key Tips for Your Child Actor:
It is sometimes hard to recognize when your agent is gatekeeping you from jobs. A red flag might be seeing a job posted that fits your criteria and not getting an audition for it. It can feel awkward to confront your agent about these things, but it is important to have all the information.

Do not be afraid to question your agent. They are not your boss, and you are not theirs. You are partners, and you should be able to come to each other with your concerns in a professional manner, and without conflict. If they are a good agent and are not trying to hold you back, they will simply explain their decisions. Use your judgment when dealing with these situations, and if you feel that a particular agent does not have your best interest in mind, then it might be time to find another one.

CHAPTER 11

The Great Agent

It may take time to find the right agent for your child. It is important to ask around and see what agent other actors have. Ask their opinions and ask others in the industry who they recommend. When you find one who fits well with your child and gives them the opportunities they deserve, it is important to keep the relationship strong. Prove to them that your child is worth their time and effort in order to get auditions, especially if you know they have a big roster.

A great agent will communicate with you regularly via phone, text, and email, and they will review all your child's tapes closely. They will make sure your child knows that they believe in them. They will recommend classes and be invested in your child's career. They will give you advice on your child's headshots and make sure they are current.

A great agent will assist your child with their resume and ensure it is kept up to date.

A great agent will communicate with you about their work with your child. They will go through your child's contracts thoroughly and ensure they get paid appropriately. They will vouch for things that you want included and are comfortable with and make sure it is on paper.

It is worth it to make sure your child has the best agent. Do not stay with an agent out of fear that breaking that contract will affect your child's career. It will not as long as you remain professional while ending a contract with said agent. There are many reputable agents and agencies to choose from.

CHAPTER 12
Training and Experience

Typically, no specific training is required to be an actor. However, it is beneficial for your child to participate in various training opportunities regularly to build their skills and abilities.

There are many ways your child can access training or gain experience. Most experienced actors offer workshops that can be taken over a weekend and focus on specific topics (e.g., set etiquette) depending on if your child is just starting out or if your child wants to further enhance their skills. These workshops are typically facilitated by acting studios. Some acting studios can also assist with resume writing, finding an agent, and creating self-tapes, and some offer general coaching.

Your child can learn a lot through experience as well. Many young actors start gaining experience in high school or community plays. Some gain experience through small parts, whether paid or unpaid, or working as an extra on set.

For more formal training, your child can attend programs in acting, theatre, or drama at school or at many colleges and universities.

The options are limitless, and it is important for a young actor to take the time to train and gain experience, so they understand the film industry and are ready to enter it. Your child will be much more successful if they learn as much as they can prior to being cast in professional roles.

CHAPTER 13

Mental Preparation and Confidence Building

An actor requires strong mental preparation and confidence for the work that they do. Mental preparation helps an actor cope with the stress of performing and handle the outcomes of their work.

An actor can do many different things to mentally prepare and help themselves cope with the highs and lows of acting.

Setting realistic short- and long-term goals helps actors establish a path toward specific milestones and maintain their targeted focus. You can assist your child actor in this, but as they mature, they must take on this responsibility themselves.

Mental imagery can also help your child actor develop and improve their mental skills. In their mind, your child can run through various scenes to rehearse their roles before any physical performances.

It is important to teach your child to relax in advance of filming. Your child may want to set up a routine to help themselves. They can start with having a good night's sleep prior to the day of filming. This could be followed with waking early, eating breakfast, arriving on set early, and warming up prior to their performance.

Some say self-confidence is the mark of a champion. Self-confidence is a positive mental attitude that can keep your child actor working hard regardless of how many times they fail to land a role. Self-confidence can give your child the courage and focus to keep trying and plays a key role in how well your child can perform. If your child is prepared, they will be more confident. Confidence can come from knowing you have trained and practised long and hard.

You should encourage your child not to compare themselves to anyone else. There will always be other actors who your child thinks are better than them. Encourage your child to focus only on themselves and on what they can control.

Encourage your child to focus on the positive and to get in the habit of looking at the upside of things. By being positive, your child will feel better about themselves and perform at a higher level. Encourage them to learn from the challenges, then let them go.

CHAPTER 14

Diversity, Inclusion, and Indigenous Representation

Many organizations talk about diversity and inclusion in the workplace today, but their actions and the way they implement their initiatives do not always match what they say. This is true as well for the film industry.

Historically, the film industry has not represented many racial or ethnic groups. Also, women of colour have been underrepresented in lead roles. It is even more difficult for Indigenous people. Not only have they been underrepresented in films, but they have also been misrepresented. In earlier years, Western films included the bulk of Indigenous representation on screen, and Indigenous peoples were often depicted just as "savages." Even now it is rare to find film and television with an Indigenous character, let alone one that is positive and well-rounded.

Given that Olivia is Indigenous and a woman, I work extra hard to make sure she knows I believe in her and her success. If your child is from a minority ethnic group, it is important first to let them know they can do anything they set their mind to. It will be necessary to build their confidence early because it will be that much more important when they go to auditions and are on film sets. They are starting from a disadvantaged position and will need to work extra hard to persevere within a system that may have extra barriers to overcome.

Olivia's Key Tips for Your Child Actor:
These days, there is much more recognition about the importance of authentic casting. Indigenous people are finding more and more opportunities to play a variety of roles in film. The need for diverse background actors and crew is also growing.

However, in many cases, advertisements are recruiting Indigenous people and saying no acting experience is required. Many Indigenous actors then sign up with little knowledge of their rights on set and are then taken advantage of. They may be working long hours, not being given appropriate breaks and meals, and being paid low wages.

If you are an Indigenous person and are new to acting, connect with other experienced Indigenous actors to find out more about your rights. Know your worth, and do not agree to anything less than what you deserve.

CHAPTER 15
Casting Calls

TRIGGER WARNING: mentions of luring, nudity, and assaults.

Actors find jobs through casting calls. Casting calls are notices made to the public or directly to casting agencies announcing that actors are required for an upcoming film production. Anyone from a student filmmaker to a major motion picture studio can issue a casting call. This notice can take place in many forms: word of mouth, online bulletin boards, online platforms, and agent notifications.

An experienced actor will get their casting call opportunities from their agent. Established agents have strong relationships with major casting agencies, production companies, directors, studios, and other industry insiders that send out calls. It is the agent's job to find the best parts for their clients.

Sometimes casting notices are generic. Other times they are very specific in terms of age, gender, height, build, race, and any special skills or talent needed.

Once a casting call is shared, your child's agent will decide to submit them or not. This is why I emphasized earlier that you need to have an agent who you can trust and who knows your child and strongly believes in their capabilities.

If it is a publicly shared casting call, you can also submit your child's resume yourself if you think the role is something your child wants to audition for. If you decide to do that, it is important to let your child's agent know. Alternatively, you can send the casting call to your agent and ask that they submit for you. Typically, a casting director will respond back to whoever submitted and make the contract with them. If you want the process to go through your agent, it is best to have them submit for your child.

Most casting calls are legitimate. Over time, you will know what key components make a casting call legitimate. However, some people conduct false casting calls to lure children into doing inappropriate things that require nudity or partial nudity. Many young people pursue acting, and sometimes deceitful people try to take advantage of this fact.

They ask actors to submit pictures of themselves, and then the false casting calls may be conducted in someone's apartment or home. Sadly, some end in assaults or worse. A good way to keep your child safe is to avoid responding to small, inexpensive ads that require any form of nudity.

Pay close attention to the details of casting calls and do not be afraid to ask questions. Trust your intuition, and if something does not feel right, then do not move forward with it.

CHAPTER 16

People Who Think They Are Important and Famous

TRIGGER WARNING: mentions of luring, nudity, and assaults.

In July 2017, I replied to an international talent search for teenage film actors. The director was planning to make a feature film in Greece. Since Olivia also has a Greek background, I thought she might be suitable for the role.

The director emailed me, asking if he could discuss the opportunity with me further. He said he was very interested in working with Olivia. He also sent me a link to a video of himself being interviewed about a feature film that he directed. He said it was nominated by a film society as Best Exposé and Best Film on Human Rights.

I sent him my phone number, and we had a quick chat. He told me he required more pictures of Olivia before he decided. He said this after I had already sent him her headshot, resume, Facebook page, website, IMDb, and demo reel. I could not help but think this was an odd request.

I decided to conduct more research on this person first before I sent him any more pictures. The best way to research individuals is to type their names into Google search on the internet and hit "enter." Numerous links to different sources of information will be provided about the individual.

I typed in the director's name, and to my dismay, I found articles on the internet about how this director and his producer tried to take advantage of a fifteen-year-old girl while casting her in a film. According to the article, the director lured her by promising to make her a star in a twelve-million-dollar feature film. The director and producer represented a film production company in Canada but had been in another country for this film.

The article stated that the young girl's mother was representing her at the time. She signed a contract that clearly stated that her daughter would not undress or be placed in indecent circumstances during the film. The film script she was given was also clean and had no indication of indecent activities for the film.

The article shared that the girl and her mother met with the director and producer in an apartment. There was another young girl there. The director asked the mother to leave so she would not intimidate the girls as they acted. The mother left the house, and that was when the director and producer sexually assaulted the girls.

Both the director and producer denied the allegations and instead insisted that the girl was not ready for the role and was making false charges about them out of revenge. I did not find anything about the outcome of this situation.

I decided to try and clear this up with the director before doing anything else. I sent him an email and told him that before I sent him any more pictures of Olivia, I had some questions. I explained that I did not mean any disrespect and that it was obvious that he was successful in the film industry. However, as Olivia's mother, it was my role to protect her first as the industry could be harsh on young girls sometimes. I explained that I always did background checks on people interested in working with Olivia. I told him that I did a few searches on him and his agency and found some questionable articles. I included the links to the articles I found. I also told him Olivia works extremely hard to be successful in the industry, but she would not do it at the risk of being harmed in any way. We would not compromise for promises of fame and fortune in the future. I asked him to provide me with reassurance that the claims in the articles were not legitimate.

He responded within a few hours and told me that he believed I was a great mother to Olivia, but that I was a very bad agent because I did not know the film industry. He said I was clearly not used to dealing with people who reached importance and fame in the industry. He said if Olivia had a real agent, considering the contract he would have given her, this could have been one of the happiest days of her life. He said my concerns made it impossible for us to work together and that our correspondence was over.

It was obvious through his reaction that he was not a nice person and not someone I wanted to leave my daughter alone with.

I was relieved that I was able to address this situation and avoid anything bad from happening. Like the mother in the article, I too was representing my daughter, who was only sixteen years old at the time.

It does not matter if a director is "famous," nothing should ever compromise your child's safety. Always do your own background checks and familiarize yourself with the people who will be working with your child. It is even more critical to do your research in a situation like this because you and your child would be in another country with people you do not really know or trust. The laws around sexual assault and other related matters may be different than where you live. Also, you may not have any support around you that you can easily turn to. Be extra careful exposing your child to any international opportunities, and ensure your child always has a guardian with them.

CHAPTER 17
The Perfect Casting Call

I saw an advertised casting call for a short film that required a number of different roles. The film was being made in celebration of Canada's 150th birthday. I sent an email to the producer with Olivia's resume and headshot, letting them know she was interested.

I received an email back with information on where and when the audition was taking place. The email also clearly stated that if an actor was under the age of eighteen, a parent or guardian must accompany them. It also stated that I should contact them if there were any issues with the date and time so they could try to accommodate the actor. I appreciated that they were very clear upfront about minors, and that they also wanted to accommodate individuals to ensure everyone that was interested had an opportunity to participate.

My experience was that they were very thoughtful and encouraging, not just to my daughter, but to me as well. I was not sure if Olivia needed to prepare anything in advance, so I sent an email to check. One of the producers of the project immediately sent me a response letting me know that the audition would be a cold reading. The producer told me the lines would be easy and straightforward. They also suggested that Olivia look at all the roles they were casting for and decide which roles she was most interested in before the audition. She would have an opportunity to try out for various roles and might be asked to be part of more than one project.

The producer then asked if I would be interested too and encouraged me to submit my own headshot and provide some information about myself. They wanted as much diversity as possible to represent true Canadians in the short film. Unfortunately, I was not able to take Olivia to the audition myself as I was travelling for work. Perry, Olivia's dad, took her there instead. While there, they asked Perry to stand by Olivia as she said her lines.

After the audition, the producer sent an email thanking everyone who made it out to the casting call. They also shared that they would be making final decisions in the next few days.

A few days later, I received an email from the producer letting us know that Olivia and Perry were both selected for the short film. They thought both Olivia and her father would be perfect for the roles of a young girl and her parent, and they said they would do their best to ensure the shoot did not conflict with Olivia's school schedule.

I was so impressed by the producers of this short film. They were so respectful, open, and accommodating. It was also a pleasant surprise to have Perry selected alongside Olivia to work on this project. They now have wonderful memories of their time on set together and laugh about how Perry booked a role too with Olivia.

CHAPTER 18

Auditions

After your child's information has been submitted for a casting call, they may receive an invite for an audition. The invite usually comes in the form of an email and goes to your child's agent. Your child's agent will contact you right away with all the details and ask you to confirm so they can respond by the deadline.

It is also important to look at the details and check when filming will take place. Make sure your child can commit to the dates and times. You do not want to waste the time of the casting director and others by having them audition for something they may not be available for.

Take a close look at the details of the audition. The casting director will have outlined the specific self-tape instructions, a breakdown of what is being filmed and where, who is directing and producing, information on all the characters, and any special instructions needed to be followed in advance of submitting. An audition can be done by submitting a self-tape or attending in person.

Keep a journal of your child's auditions and take notes about what they wore to each audition, as well as other decisions that were made about the performance. You will need this information if your child is asked for a callback.

CHAPTER 19

The Adult Film Producer

In January 2016 I submitted Olivia's resume for a role in a feature film for the first time. I received a response saying, "Thank you for your interest in our upcoming feature film and for bringing Olivia to our attention. We have reviewed her information, and I, or one of our producers, will be contacting you for an audition soon."

We were so excited that Olivia was invited for an audition but were also nervous as this would be her first time auditioning in front of a producer. Her audition date was set for February 2016, and it was to be done in person and at a set location.

We received the script, and Olivia and I read it in advance to better understand the character and the scenes. Olivia then practised all her lines. It is important to learn as many of the lines as possible. Actors are allowed to take their script into the audition with them, but it is best to show that you are prepared and do not need it.

While Olivia worked on her lines, I decided to research the director and the film to find further information. I was surprised to find out that the director was an adult film (i.e., pornographic) producer, and this was his first non-pornographic film involving teenagers.

I did not know what to think at first, and I did not know if I should tell Olivia. How could I say something and ruin her first ever audition for a feature film? I read the script and did not have any initial concerns as it seemed very appropriate for her age.

I decided to tell Olivia in the car on the way to the audition. I wanted to make sure she was aware, and we talked about how to stay safe knowing that once she was at the audition, she would go into the audition room without me.

When Olivia first started auditioning, I would go into the building with her and wait outside the audition room, especially since she was a minor. She preferred me not to be in the audition room with her, but I encourage you to go in the room with your child if they are comfortable with you being there. As Olivia grew older and became more experienced, I would wait in the car outside the building.

In this case, I waited outside the room in the front entrance lobby. The audition took no longer than fifteen minutes. Olivia shared what happened once we were in the car driving home. She had to act out the lines in front of a

THE ADULT FILM PRODUCER

couple of producers while being recorded on camera. Once she had finished acting out the lines, she was allowed to leave. Producers and casting directors do not give any feedback at the auditions. No one does at any time.

As we drove home, we could not help but laugh a little about the fact that she just auditioned for an adult film producer at the age of fifteen, although we recognized that this film was not an adult film. The film looked legitimate and was casting mostly for teenagers, so I was comfortable with her moving forward. However, I was still cautious.

Olivia was offered a small role in the film, and I had an opportunity to email the producer and get reassurance that she would be kept safe. He said, "This is the first time I have worked with such young actors, so I wanted to make it as comfortable for them as possible. We will be inviting the parents of any actors under eighteen to be present on set. I also have an amazing crew who will go out of their way to make everyone feel as welcome and safe as possible, and I know this because I have seen them do it on several previous projects."

This was a positive experience for Olivia. She had a small role in this feature film and gained valuable work experience. The director was kind and responsive and answered all my questions respectfully and in a professional manner. Regardless, at the end of the day, it was important and well worth it to be aware of who she was working for and to ensure her safety.

Always do your own research on whatever film your child may be working on. There are many resources on the internet that allow you to do this.

CHAPTER 20

Self-Tapes

Many actors today submit self-tapes for auditions. A self-tape is a pre-recorded video audition that is sent to a casting director. Actors must film themselves acting out select portions of a script. Usually, the audition request will lay out all the directions on what must be filmed and how to pull the self-tape together. The film must be sent in electronically before the deadline.

If your child plans to act as much as possible, it is wise to invest in the proper tools for filming self-tapes. You will need a good camera, although most cell phone cameras work well. You will also need good lighting and a room that is clear and free of background noise. You can film against a plain white wall, but most actors will use a solid blue background. I purchased photography lights and a background kit. I also went to the local fabric store and purchased blue material that we could hang on any wall. I highly recommend this because you can take it with you while travelling. Your child can be called to audition at any time, and it is good to be prepared.

When filming a self-tape, your child will need you or someone else to read the lines for the other characters in the script. Whoever is reading the additional lines should do this off-camera.

There are some general rules about self-tapes:
- Always film them against a wall or plain backdrop.
- Only film your child saying their lines. The other reader can be off camera, both reading and operating the camera.
- Stick to the script, and do not change the lines.
- Do not add in any extra pieces that you think may enhance the script.

All self-tapes also require a slate. A slate is when an actor introduces themselves. The audition details will lay out what must be included in a slate, but often it is your child's name, height, and where they are located. If your child is under eighteen years, they must also state their age. Once your child is eighteen, they no longer need to share their age. Most casting directors will request a full body shot as well.

Watching an actor's slate is usually the first moment the casting director sees your child outside of their headshot or demo reel, so it is important to make a good first impression. It is important for your child to show their confidence, personality, and anything else that makes them stand out.

CHAPTER 21

Fun at the Park

When Olivia received her first request for a self-tape, it was just after we came back from the talent event in Florida. We did not know much about how to submit a self-tape.

I googled self-tapes on the internet and watched a few but did not give them a lot of thought. My initial reaction was that they were weird because the actors were just standing and talking in front of a plain wall behind them.

Olivia and I decided that we would make her self-tapes more interesting. I do not think anyone could mess up a self-tape as much as we did in that moment.

The role that Olivia was reading for was a cheerleader in a ball field. Olivia and I decided to go to our local park and film the scene there.

As we were filming, Olivia decided that the lines sounded stupid and that girls her age would never say those things. So, we decided to just change the lines in the script using language that Olivia thought would be more appropriate.

We also decided to end the self-tape with Olivia doing cartwheels across the grass while funky music played in the background.

I was so proud of the self-tape when I sent it to the casting director. The only reply I received was "Please do this over—here is a link to an example of a self-tape." Obviously, we had not made an appropriate self-tape. I was so embarrassed once we realized we should not have done that. But afterward, Olivia and I laughed so much, and I still laugh every time I see the video.

The process for creating self-tapes is very prescriptive and should not be changed. Once your child is familiar with how they must be done, it becomes easier, and they will learn to work within the parameters that must be followed.

There are plenty of examples online of good self-tapes that your child can use as a guide.

CHAPTER 22
The Script, or Sides

When your child is invited for an audition, the casting company will send the script, or sides, to your agent for the audition.

Your child's agent will send you all the information about the audition and attach the script. Your child will only receive a portion of the script that pertains to the character they will be reading for.

It is acceptable for your child to take the script into the audition, but again, it is best if they do not read from it directly. Still, your child may need the script if they forget any of their lines and want to refresh their memory.

Sometimes your child may receive a script with only one line. The other characters in the script may have the bulk of the lines. The script may be a particular scene, and the casting director may be looking for your child's ability to react. Other times your child may receive a long script with more than one scene.

It is important that your child not just memorize the lines, but really try to understand the character and figure out the best way to act out the scene(s). Keep in mind that every actor auditioning is reading the same words over and over. It is up to your child actor to interpret and express the words in an original and interesting way and to make the character their own.

Your child should take time to break down the script and understand what is happening in each scene. Your child should try to connect to the scene. They could imagine themselves in the same situation and portray how they would react.

Olivia and I would sit down and discuss the scenes and the characters. We would make sure we both read the script a couple of times, and then we would discuss what we thought the scenes were about. We talked about what the tone would be like and practised going over the lines together in different ways. She would read for her character, and I would read all the other lines in the script. Sometimes there are multiple characters. You do not need to change your voice for each character. The agent is not paying attention to you as a background reader, only your child.

When Olivia first started doing auditions, we did not put as much time into preparing in advance. We jumped into filming right away. Now we make sure that Olivia has

THE SCRIPT, OR SIDES

time to learn the scripts, think about how best to present the characters, and lay out each scene prior to filming, including deciding on what she should wear and how she should look.

CHAPTER 23

Callbacks

If a casting director likes your child's audition or self-tape, your child may be asked for a callback. A callback is an invitation to return for a second audition.

There are some important things to remember if you want your child to be successful at the callback. Since your child did well at the first audition, they should try to do the same things again. Remember that earlier, I told you to keep notes; now review those notes about what your child wore to the audition and other decisions they made about the performance. Also review your child's self-tape as a reminder of how your child performed. Only audition for a new scene if your child is specifically directed to do so.

There may be new people in the room, including producers. Your child may also be asked to read with other actors who are already part of the film, which they call a chemistry read. Tell your child to try not to be intimidated and stay focused on their role.

After your child has completed a callback, take time to treat yourselves. Regardless of whether your child gets the role, it is important to acknowledge how far your child went in the process and celebrate this achievement.

CHAPTER 24
No Response

Your child will go to many auditions and will often not hear back from anyone again. If the casting director has not selected your child, you will not get any further information on the audition.

This is not always related to how your child acted. Your child may have done an amazing job and walked out feeling great and thinking that for certain they had landed the role, but the directors might not select them for reasons that are out of your control. Sometimes your child may be too short, be too tall, not have the hair colour or skin tone the director is looking for, be better suited for a different role, etc.

The role that your child auditioned for is also one part of a bigger picture. It is the casting director's job to look at all the roles—all the pieces within that bigger picture—and cast them to fit together.

It is best to encourage your child to walk away from an audition, to not overthink each role, and to not take the rejection personally. Each audition is an opportunity for your child to build new skills, learn from the process, and challenge themselves to continue to expand their abilities.

After an audition takes place, it is hard because you want to focus on what will happen if your child is successful in the role. But it can also be a real disappointment if you wait and never hear anything back. This happens in most auditions and is a normal part of the process.

It is important that you prepare your child as early as you can to move on from one audition to the next. After an audition, whether your child feels it went well or not so well, it is good to quickly debrief. It is a good time to also celebrate your child's hard work and determine what they may want to do better next time.

It is not a great idea to get fixated on the role and become anxious about hearing back. The best thing is to walk away, reassuring your child that they have done the best job they could at the time and that it was a great experience. If your child happens to get the role, that would be a bonus.

It is difficult to understand sometimes why one person is chosen over another. Remember again that many times, that decision may not have to do with your child's acting skills.

NO RESPONSE

The audition process also allows actors to meet casting directors and build their networks so that when the next big thing comes up, they are memorable.

CHAPTER 25

Landing a Role

Once your child has completed an audition and even a callback, do not expect to hear back unless your child has landed the role. Usually, if your child has successfully been chosen for a role, the casting director will notify your child's agent. You may sometimes hear back quickly, or you may not hear back for several weeks or even months.

It is not unusual to hear back a few months later. Sometimes you may think that your child was not successful, and you have moved on to other things. Then you get a pleasant surprise that your child was selected. There is no set deadline for notifying actors. Also, there are no rules saying that a casting director must let an actor know if they were successful or not.

When an offer is made to your child, they are typically asked to sign a nondisclosure agreement (NDA). An NDA is an agreement signed by an actor that stops them from sharing any information about the film project and their involvement in it. This includes ensuring the actor does not announce anything, post anything on social media, or talk about the film to anyone. If an actor does not want to sign the NDA, they are not likely to be given the offer, as confidentiality in the filming industry is taken very seriously and can ruin your child's career if broken. The NDA will typically have an end date, and it will be important to pay attention to the details of the agreement and follow them closely.

Sometimes your child may be bound not to disclose anything about a film they are working on for months or even years. It may be hard for you as a proud parent not to share details with your close friends and family members, especially if they are aware your child works in the film industry. Family and friends like to ask about your children and are always curious about what your child actor is working on. When others ask me about Olivia's projects, I usually reply with broad and general information, such as "She is working on a feature film right now" and "I don't know much about it, as I am not on set."

In addition to signing an NDA, your child will also receive a written offer. The offer will include outside shoot dates. The outside dates are when a film will start and stop filming. This does not mean your child will be working for that whole period, but it does mean your child is committing to those dates and will make themselves available during that time frame if they need your child on set.

The offer will also include the amount of pay your child will receive and any other benefits, such as travel and accommodations if the filming is taking place in another city. The offer may also include any special arrangements that your agent may have worked out with the production team.

It is important to get a written offer signed and agreed to ahead of filming to ensure your child understands and commits to the agreed-upon parameters of the job.

If your child is a minor, then you as the parent must sign the agreement on behalf of your child. If your child's agent is their power of attorney, they can also sign it on their behalf. Make sure you review the offer and NDA thoroughly before signing.

CHAPTER 26

It Is Okay to Say No

If your child is fortunate to be invited to play a role in a film and chooses not to participate, that is okay too. It is important not to force your child to play a role they may not be comfortable with. You should never feel like you cannot say no for fear that this would impact your child's future opportunities.

Olivia was once offered a small role in a film without auditioning, and when she found out what it was about, she did not want to do it. At first, I tried to encourage her, and then I realized that she firmly did not want to do the part. At the end of the day, it was her choice to make, not mine.

I felt bad telling the director that she did not want to take the role. I was afraid this might impact her in the future. I discussed this with her acting coach at the time, and he said that an actor should not compromise their own personal integrity. He also reassured me that turning down a small role like that was okay because it probably would not have advanced her career. He also said there would always be lots of films being made and she would get other opportunities in the future.

It is important to allow your child to decide on their own what their personal standards and preferences are. They should have a clear idea of what they will or will not do. When it comes time for your child to make a choice about their roles, they should be able to do so with confidence and ease.

CHAPTER 27
Olivia's First Callback

I will never forget Olivia's first big callback. It was on a winter day following a major snowstorm. It was also the day when I was involved in my first ever car accident. Fortunately, my vehicle was not damaged too much, but the poor car that rear ended me in the intersection was badly damaged. I was so startled by the accident that I was afraid to drive, and it took me a few hours to calm down.

We had committed to driving from Edmonton to Calgary for this callback, and it was a three-hour drive in the aftermath of the snowstorm. Sometimes when you know how big of an opportunity it is for your child, you just do it, hoping the results will be positive.

Olivia and I drove to Calgary that afternoon, and we overnighted in a hotel. Olivia spent the evening preparing. The callback was for a popular television series with a strong fan base. If she was to get the role, she would be filming over a six-month period and be in several episodes. It was a significant role, so it was worth the effort to commit.

Olivia had the opportunity at the callback to audition with the star of the show. This tends to happen with callbacks as the producers want to see the chemistry between the actors.

I watched Olivia enter the building as I waited in the car. I also watched the star of the show drive up, park her car, and walk into the building. It was a surreal moment; I thought about how far my girl had come and how close she was to landing a role in a major television show.

I wanted this so badly for her, but she was not selected for the role. She did receive some great feedback, though, which is unusual. The casting director said that Olivia had a good callback audition, but they decided to go with another actor. They said she needed to work on really breaking down the scenes line by line and being very specific with each moment. They said that listening well was better than trying to anticipate what was coming next.

They also said that they really liked her and would try to find another role for her that season as they absolutely loved how confident she was.

It was a wonderful experience for both of us. I could not have been prouder of her for getting this far in the process. Just having the experience and learning from it was so beneficial. I knew her day would come, and this was just another opportunity to move her further along in the process.

CHAPTER 28

The Contract

It is so exciting when your child lands a role, especially in a prominent film, that you sometimes do not pay as much attention to the fine details of a contract. I highly recommend you always pay attention to the fine details of any contract, regardless of its stature.

A contract is a written agreement between your child actor and the client, who will be their employer throughout the acting job. This is a legally binding document, and it is meant to protect the interests of both parties involved. The contract lays out all the detailed terms and conditions needed to complete an acting job.

It is a good idea to write down all the standard requirements for your child in advance of any role so you can use it as a template for reviewing contracts.

A release form is included in most contracts, but it may be an additional separate legal document that you must sign for your child actor. The release form is a document that your child may be required to sign agreeing that the film company will own the rights to their performance in the film. This means that your child will not own the rights to any of the parts in the project they performed in.

A standard contract will contain a detailed description of the work, the outside dates of the film, and the days and times within the outside dates your child actor will be required to work.

The contract will also lay out the payment conditions. The pay will depend on whether it is a union shoot or a non-union shoot. If your child is a member of a union, then there are certain pay scales that must be followed by an employer. If your child is not part of a union, then you may have some say in how much your child gets paid unless the shoot advertised certain rates when casting. However, it is always wise to discuss payment options early on in a contract agreement as it is important to ensure your child actor is getting sufficient pay and you are satisfied with the rates.

The contract should also include a section on expenses. This usually includes coverage for things like food, travel, and accommodations, if required.

It is important to review any clauses about the termination of a contract by one or both parties. The clause should include reasons for early termination and who is responsible if one party decides to break the contract. A breach of contract would be considered serious, and you would need to involve a lawyer to deal with it if it were to happen.

Typically, it is the role of your child's agent to review the contracts and ensure your child is properly compensated and protected. However, it is still important for you to double-check everything.

CHAPTER 29

Preparations Before Filming

Prior to filming, your child will need to participate in rehearsals. They may also do table reads, where actors and the production team sit together and read the script aloud for the first time so everyone gets a feel for what it will be like on set and can prepare themselves in advance. Your child will also go to fittings, hair, and makeup. These are done in advance to prepare for filming.

During rehearsals, your child will have an opportunity to practise their lines, meet the other actors, and discuss each of the scenes together. This is a great opportunity to prepare for being on set and becoming more comfortable with the scenes.

If your child is working on a smaller film production, sometimes the expectation is that your child will bring their own clothes for filming. Usually, you will receive guidance in advance on what their outfits should look like. If you do not hear from them, make sure you ask, so your child is ready to go once on set.

When filming is about to start, your child will receive a call sheet the day before filming. The call sheet will include all the details of what to expect on set, such as who will be on set, what time your child must arrive, the order of scenes being shot, mealtimes, filming locations, end times, etc.

For smaller productions, actors must find their own way to and from filming sets. If your child is in a big-budget film, they may be fortunate enough to have transportation provided.

It is a good idea to bring something with you for your child to do while waiting on set. You do not want your child to get too distracted, as it will cause them to lose concentration at work.

It is like any other job, so your child should keep all their conversations professional. If they want to have a personal relationship with the actors they meet, they should do it outside of work.

Your child will spend more time sitting and waiting than filming. Your child will need to be ready to get up and go as soon as they are called.

CHAPTER 30

Filming

Once your child arrives on set, they will typically go straight to makeup for makeup and hair. Depending on the film, your child will either show up in their outfit for filming, or they will go to wardrobe next and get their outfit.

Then your child will go and block the scenes with the director and other actors. For example, they will lay out where your child is going to walk, sit, look, talk, etc., and determine what camera angles to use.

Once that is done, your child will begin filming. The scenes are shot repeatedly at different angles. Your child will do multiple takes and may have a break in between setups. Your child will typically film a scene until the director is happy with the filmed scene.

If your child is filming multiple scenes that day, your child will get breaks between scenes. The breaks allow your child to run through their lines again, get to know their scene partners, fix makeup, change wardrobe, eat, etc.

Keep in mind that how your child envisions a scene is not usually how it is shot. Directors can change the lines during filming, and your child needs to be prepared to switch it up and not be fixed on the script.

If it is your child's first time filming, or if your child is nervous, tell them to find time to go to the bathroom or find a quiet space to run through their lines aloud.

Your child should also take advantage of craft services if they are available on set. Craft services provides food and beverages. It will be important for your child to get good rest, eat well, and not be thirsty before and during filming.

Some days, filming is short and easy, but other days, it can be long and tiring. The main thing about the long days is to ensure that your child stays professional and does not complain unnecessarily.

It is important to know the rights of your child actor. There are certain rules that must be followed under the union depending on what area you live in. Make sure you understand the rules in your jurisdiction in order to protect your child from being taken advantage of.

Parents must be on set with minors while filming. Even if it is not a union shoot, it is best for parents to stay on set to ensure their child is safe.

FILMING

If your child is filming during school time, make sure you talk to your child's teacher about the fact that this is a great opportunity for your child and that you hope they are supportive too. Explain how you will need to take your child out of school for filming and discuss ways your child can keep up with their schoolwork.

If your child is filming for a longer period, check the union rules, because they may be entitled to have a tutor to help with schoolwork.

Make sure that your child has time to balance acting with other parts of their life.

Your child will need time to focus on school. Although your child may seem determined to have a career in acting, they may change their mind later in life. Your child will need a strong educational foundation for whatever they pursue. A strong education will also assist your child to better understand the film industry and be more professional.

Your child should have time to spend with their friends or family while growing up. Your child may also want to pursue other interests or hobbies.

CHAPTER 31
Different Types of Films

There are different types of films your child may participate in.

Short Films ("Shorts")
When starting out, the most common type of film that your child may act in is a short film. A short film is usually a minimum of five minutes and does not exceed thirty. It is referred to as a "short" and is mostly made by new filmmakers. They are important because they allow your child to practise all their filmmaking skills.

There are lots of opportunities to participate in short films at film schools. Students who are studying filmmaking need to make short films as part of their assignments and are always looking for actors.

Short films can sometimes take as long or even longer to make than feature films. It really depends on what the film is about and how the director wants to shoot it. Olivia was in a short film that took a year and a half to make because the director wanted to film at different locations in Alberta and during different seasons.

Feature Films
Although similar to short films, feature films have some distinct differences. Of course, a feature film will be longer than a short film and may have to meet certain length requirements. A feature film also requires a bigger budget as film costs will be greater, including equipment needs, wardrobe and film crew, etc.

Television Series
Any program on television that continues through episodes is referred to as a television series. This could include things like dramas, reality shows, and game shows. The episodes usually form an ongoing story rather than many self-contained stories.

Promotional Films
Companies use promotional films to promote their products or services to customers. These are like commercials. However, commercials are broadcast through television or online. Promotional videos are longer and more in-depth,

DIFFERENT TYPES OF FILMS

and they provide more information about a product or service.

Commercials

Companies use commercials to try to sell their products or services to people. Commercials are shorter and more focused on grabbing a viewer's attention. Commercials create memorable and persuasive messages to encourage people to buy company products or services.

CHAPTER 32

Olivia's First Commercial

In September 2019, Olivia auditioned for her first commercial. Because it was for a brand-new company, it had a smaller budget, paying only $450 per actor for a day's work.

The role was for an unimpressed "goth" daughter, and the commercial would be airing for one year online and on TV.

Olivia was booked (officially cast) for the role. Prior to filming, she was given a production schedule with a breakdown of all the scenes and when they would be filmed during the day. The schedule also included the address of the location that filming would take place.

There were also instructions for wardrobe. Olivia was required to bring three outfits as options, but only two would be used. The clothes needed to be black with some white stripes underneath as accents. Hair and makeup were provided on set.

While filming, the director decided to film two different scenes to allow for two commercials.

Olivia won a Joey Award (awarded to young Canadian actors) as Best Actress in a Commercial 12-17 Years for her role in this commercial.

Although Olivia enjoyed her role in the commercial, it was not the area of acting that she was interested in. She wanted to focus mainly on feature films or television series.

There are some people that love to just do commercials, and that is okay too. What is most important is allowing your child to focus on whatever they are interested in doing.

CHAPTER 33

Knowing Your Own Worth

Olivia was working on a film set that had several challenges. The work environment was poor, and the cast and crew were very unhappy, including Olivia. She decided that it was so toxic she could not continue until the issues were addressed. So, she stood up for herself and her work colleagues and brought their concerns to her agent and the union. There were other actors who did the same, and the production was eventually shut down due to the many voiced concerns.

Everyone, especially your child, deserves to be treated with respect while on the job. This should never, ever be compromised. Respect is one of the most important behaviours in the workplace because it creates a positive work culture for everyone.

A respectful attitude should be the standard in any workplace. When your child is on set, they may already be experiencing some anxiety or stress because they want to ensure they do a great job. If a work environment is not respectful, it can add additional unnecessary stress onto your child and make it harder for them to concentrate on their role.

It was probably one of the lowest moments for Olivia in her career and led us to a heart-to-heart discussion. In the seven years since she had first started her acting career, this was the first time we both thought it was a good idea for her to take a break from acting and plan what she would do with the rest of her life. Thankfully, Olivia landed an unexpected role immediately after this happened, which encouraged her and reaffirmed for her that she should continue pursuing her dream. I am still so proud of her for standing up for herself and others on set.

Olivia's Key Tips for Your Child Actor:
Everyone should feel safe in the workplace regardless of the type of work they are doing, and no one should be victimized for speaking out. In the film industry, cast and crew are generally not encouraged to speak up if they have concerns. Whenever they do, they tend to be made out as troublemakers and difficult to work with when all they are asking for is a safe place to work. Because of the nature of the work and the ability to gain exposure while participating in films, many actors are afraid that if they speak up, they will lose out on their chance for fame, which makes it appealing to stay quiet.

KNOWING YOUR OWN WORTH

However, what many actors do not realize is that by staying quiet they would be giving up so much more. Workplace abuse has lasting effects on actors, and it can affect their ability to work in the future. It may seem risky to speak up, especially if others are not, but it is worth it. The more you speak out, the better environments become for yourself and everyone involved.

You do not owe anyone anything. Make sure you are clear about your boundaries. It is okay to walk away if you feel like your health or well-being is in danger. You can say no, and you can leave any set that makes you feel unsafe or uncomfortable. Lean on family if you need support. They would not want you to stay in that situation, and they would be more than willing to help you get out of it.

CHAPTER 34
Big Roles

Everyone in the industry is always waiting for their "big break"—the moment when they land a big role that makes them recognizable to the world. Some say that all it takes is that one role to change their life. It might seem like winning the lottery, but it does not happen by chance. The struggle to become a recognized actor is tough, and your child will need to be fully committed in order to pursue their big break as there are many other actors chasing the same dream.

You will also not know when that opportunity will happen. Sometimes it is by chance or by being in the right place at the right time. Sometimes it may happen when least expected.

Olivia just happened to have one outstanding audition after she left the toxic set of the film she was working on. At the time, she was thinking she should have declined it with her agent, but it was too late to do so. We decided she should just get it done and submit it that morning, even though she was exhausted.

Olivia and I went into my exercise room and found a blank wall we could use as we did not have a proper set up ready. We made do with what we could find in the room. I used a fold-up dinner table and a pile of old VHS tapes to form a stand, and used my regular phone for recording. After all, we just wanted to get it over with.

Olivia read her lines a few times, and then we began recording. We did three takes before Olivia decided her self-tape was good enough to submit. I asked her if she wanted to review it first, and she said no. I decided to take a quick look before sending the file to her and realized there was a stain on my wall clearly showing in the video. Embarrassed by it, I told her that we could not submit it that way. She said, "Mom, it's fine. Maybe it adds character."

I decided it did not matter anyway as Olivia was going to take a break from acting. It was not time to be fussy.

Olivia submitted that self-tape, and we went on to plan for Olivia to rest prior to going back to her home in Vancouver. We were both exhausted from her difficult experience and needed some time to decompress.

Three days later, Olivia received a call from her agent saying she was pinned for the role she just submitted for. When an actor is pinned for a role, it means the casting director and production really liked their audition, and they want the actor to hold the dates.

BIG ROLES

A few more days passed, and Olivia received another notice from her agent that she was now short listed for the role. At this point, it meant that Olivia was being considered with a few other actors for the role. Then she was sent notice that she was the one chosen, and her self-tape was being sent to the producers for final approval.

It was a surreal moment for Olivia and me. Right at one of her lowest moments, when we had just discussed her taking a break from acting to consider other careers she might have been interested in, she received this wonderful acting opportunity to be part of a high-profile series coming out on a major network channel.

The universe was clearly sending Olivia a message: it was not time to give up on her dream of being a professional actor. This was just the boost that Olivia needed to refocus and move on. As her Uncle David Anderson had so eloquently said to her a few days before, "Do not let one incident affect your dreams. There will always be someone else who will want you for another project." He was so right!

I could not help but think about all those big casting directors and producers who were seeing the audition tape with the stain running down my wall.

Within that same week, Olivia returned to Vancouver and had the most wonderful experience on set filming this role. It not only uplifted her but inspired her to continue pursuing her dream, and she was able to get past the unfortunate situation she was exposed to earlier that month.

CHAPTER 35
Typecasting

Typecasting is when an actor is chosen for similar types of roles because of their appearance or previous success in particular roles.

Sometimes typecasting is okay because once an actor knows the type of roles they want to play, they can perfect the skills necessary and be ready when a director is looking for a particular role. However, this is not always the case.

For example, Olivia is Inuvialuk (Western Arctic Inuk), and many casting directors now are looking for authentic Indigenous actors. Olivia fits the description of an Indigenous girl, with long black hair, brown eyes, and an olive skin tone. She could be easily cast in films requiring beautiful Indigenous actresses. However, when she first began acting, she told me she did not want to be typecast; she did not want to be selected for roles just because of what she looks like and can portray.

Olivia has been training to be a professional actor that can play many diverse roles. She is also known for being ethnically ambiguous and can be cast in roles of different ethnicity.

Sometimes typecasting can negatively affect a career. If an actor is always playing a certain character, they never have an opportunity to play various roles and gain substance. Over time, audiences may also start to see an actor playing similar roles over and over in different movies and lose interest. An actor can get stuck in a rut, and their training and experience may be lacking in variety.

Also consider that if, over time, your child's type is not needed anymore, roles would be hard to find. It is best to keep a variety of personalities in your child's back pocket to keep their options open.

CHAPTER 36
Demo Reels

A demo reel is a video collection of an actor's best performances and is usually between one to two minutes long. Demo reels are useful to submit to talent agents and managers when seeking representation. Your child's agent will use the demo reel to send out to casting directors searching for actors.

It is beneficial for your child to have a demo reel. If your child does not have any acting experience yet, you can pay to have a demo reel made. Some experienced actors do this as part of their business. They will provide you with age-appropriate scripts, then film, edit, and produce a reel for you. They even hire additional actors to play alongside your child for the full effect.

You can also look for opportunities to get your child cast in student films or independent films. They may pay only a small amount, but many promise to provide you with high-quality clips for your child's demo reel.

Once your child has acted in a few roles, make sure you ask the director for clips of your child's scenes. The post-production process of filmmaking takes lots of time, so you may have a long wait for the clips.

Once you have some clips, use video editing software to put them together for your child's demo reel. If you are not able to do it yourself, you can hire a video editor or ask a friend to help you.

Make sure your child's demo reel starts with their most impressive work. Include scenes where your child has the most dialogue. At the end of your child's reel, include their name, agent, contact information, and any self-promoting social media accounts your child may have.

As your child continues to act, make sure you are updating the demo reel with their latest work. Include your child's demo reel in casting calls and on any of your child's promotional sites.

CHAPTER 37

Pay

Being an actor does not necessarily amount to great pay, especially in the beginning. If anything, you will need to invest in your child to get them started in the industry. All the things that I wrote about earlier—headshots, training, demo reels—will require you to invest your own money.

At the beginning, your child may work for free just to gain some experience and get some clips for a demo reel. After a while, though, you will realize that your child has enough experience and should be getting paid more for their talent.

Actor's pay varies significantly, and there are no set rates unless your child is a member of a union. In some cases, your child may be paid a half-day rate, full-day rate, or even minimum wage.

The pay depends on the job and the film company. If your child is doing a small role for a low-budget film, they may only get paid a small amount. However, if your child is cast in a film for a big film production company, they could get paid much more.

It also takes time for your child to receive their pay. If your child has an agent, the cheque is sent to their agent first. Your child's agent will take their 10 to 15 percent share and send your child the remainder.

If your child has a manager, it would be your responsibility to pay them up to 15 percent or whatever you have agreed to.

If your child is a minor, there are laws that protect their earnings, and you will need to put aside a percentage of their pay into a trust account. For example, in the United States of America there is a well-known law called the Coogan Law, named after child actor Jackie Coogan. It ensures that when a young actor performs work under a contract, 15 percent of the gross earnings will be set aside for them until they reach legal majority.

The laws may vary depending on where you and your child actor live. It is important that you find out what the laws are in your community so you can follow them appropriately. Check with your child's union for more specific information.

Olivia worked for free early on in her acting career to gain experience and to receive movie credits. Movie credits provide her with recognition that she appeared on a film. She has also had a variety of lower- to higher-paying jobs depending on the projects she has been involved in.

PAY

There have been times that Olivia has had to wait several months to get paid after a job. The only mechanism for checking on her pay was to go through her agency and have them reach out to the company for updates. Unlike other forms of work, actors sometimes are not taken seriously or treated with the same respect after performing and completing a job.

There are no set deadlines by which actors must get paid. It is important that actors plan their finances in advance to make sure they have their basic needs met.

Taxes do not automatically come off your child's pay either. Actors must set aside a percentage of their funds to account for tax deductions, or else they may end up stuck during tax season with a large payment that must be paid back.

CHAPTER 38

Promotion

There are many ways that you can promote your child online: websites, the Internet Movie Database (IMDb), and social media are the most common. It is important that you decide how many online promotional tools you want to use because you have to manage these accounts and monitor them very carefully.

I decided to use a website, Facebook, and an IMDb account as the main ways to promote Olivia. Once Olivia was older, she set up her own Instagram page as well.

I began by establishing a website and paid for a domain name in order to use Olivia Kate Iatridis as the main address. I established the website for Olivia, and it does require ongoing work to keep it current.

I invest a lot of time into keeping her IMDb account up to date and current. The IMDb is the largest, most comprehensive movie database on the internet. It offers an extensive database of movie, TV show, and cast information. If your child has worked on a film, video, or TV show that is already listed in the database, and they received on-screen credit, they will be eligible to be listed on IMDb.

IMDb offers many features: you can add photos, videos, a short biography, agent contact information, and more. It is a great way to keep track of all the experience your child acquires throughout their acting career. However, in order to use all the wonderful features, you must pay an annual fee.

Many of my friends and family became interested in following Olivia on social media after she attended that first talent event. I was posting updates on my personal page and became overwhelmed with friend requests. I wanted to keep her information separate from mine, so I decided to set up a business page just for her. I tied her page to my personal page so I could manage it closely.

Olivia has had her Facebook page since she began acting. It is also a great record of her career highlights so far.

Given that Olivia was a minor when the page was established, it was important for me to make sure the security settings were tight. Olivia is a beautiful girl and could look older than she was. This sometimes attracted unwanted and inappropriate advances from men of all ages from around the world.

PROMOTION

Actors today need a social media presence, but it also exposes your child actor to a much bigger world, and you will need to keep them safe. There are many tips online about ways that you can do this, such as running any accounts for your child yourself, turning off your location, only posting after you have left a location, being careful with what photos you post, etc. Take a cyberbullying course with your child actor and have conversations with them about the use of social media, including what is acceptable and not. The more aware your child is about social media and the risks, the better.

CHAPTER 39
Celebrate

Over the years, as I learned more about the film industry and supported Olivia's acting career, I realized how much work goes into acting and making a film. I watched Olivia spend hours learning her lines, studying her scripts, preparing her wardrobe, waking early to do her hair and makeup, driving to jobs, and spending hours on set getting just the right scene by filming repeatedly.

I wanted Olivia to celebrate her success—no matter how big or small it was. Olivia and I created fun ways to do that. She loved to go out and eat at her favourite restaurant after every audition or when filming was done. We would sit and indulge in our favourite food as she shared all her experiences with me.

Whenever there was an opportunity to recognize Olivia for her work, I would submit for nominations to youth arts awards and young Canadian actor awards.

Sometimes the films she acted in were also submitted to various festivals, where they were nominated for different awards. One year, a short film that Olivia played a supporting role in won Audience Choice for Best Dramatic Short after it premiered for the first time in theatres.

Olivia wanted to wear a long gown to the premiere as it was her first red carpet event. We all got dressed up, and I bought extra tickets for our extended family to attend. We all went to the premiere together and celebrated her success.

Olivia also received three Joey Awards: Best Supporting or Principal Actor in a Short Film 15-16 Years, Best Actress in a Commercial Award, and Outstanding Indigenous Performer. These were all wonderful moments when we had an opportunity to celebrate her success.

CHAPTER 40
On Her Own

When Olivia turned seventeen, she graduated from high school. She was still determined to work and save enough money to move out on her own at eighteen to pursue her dream of becoming a professional actor.

By the time she was eighteen, she had saved enough to make the big move to Vancouver, Canada. She now has a wonderful agent who believes in her and submits her resume for principal roles. Olivia continues to develop her acting skills through ongoing workshops, training, and the many auditions she submits to regularly.

The best thing for me was being able to let her go knowing that I did everything I could to prepare her for the film industry. I have so many wonderful memories of the quality time we spent together.

I will continue to support Olivia as she pursues acting as a career. I assist her from afar in whatever she needs, but she is very independent and does most of the work on her own now.

Supporting your child to pursue their passion for acting early on and helping them build a strong foundation helps them succeed. I am extremely proud of Olivia and how far she has come at such a young age. I know there is so much more to come from Olivia as she continues to grow in the film industry. I cannot wait to write about the next phase in her career.

Glossary

Olivia's Top Fifty Terms

actor – A person who acts out the part of a character in a film.

agent – A person who represents an actor and manages any of the business, financial, or contractual matters on their behalf.

agency – An organization established to provide a particular service related to actors.

audition – A short performance that an actor gives in order to show that they are suitable for a particular role.

block the scenes – When a director works with the actors to figure out their movements, body positions, and body language prior to filming a scene.

breakdown – A document that contains important information about the production elements of a film, including the roles being cast for that film.

buyout – A lump sum that is paid upfront to actors in lieu of receiving residuals whenever a film or commercial airs. It is a one-time payment only.

booked – To be officially cast in a role. An actor is not officially cast until they accept an offer for work and receive the details.

boom – An overhead microphone, usually on an extended pole.

callback – An invitation from a film production to return for a second audition.

call sheet – A document sent out to the cast and crew that outlines where they need to be for the following shoot day. It also outlines the schedule for the day and other important details.

call time – The exact time that an actor is due to be on the set.

casting call – A notice made to the public or to casting agencies that actors are required for an upcoming production. It is a process used to select certain type of actors for roles.

casting director – The person responsible for choosing the cast who will fill the roles in a film production.

character – A person or other being in a story that is being filmed and are usually the core of a movie.

cold read – Reading aloud from a script with no practice in advance.

commission – The percentage of the actor's earnings, usually between 10 to 15 percent as per industry standards, that agents or managers charge as a fee for their services.

craft services – The area that provides cast and crew with snacks, drinks, and food while they are working.

GLOSSARY

credits – A recognition list that appears on screen of people who have participated in a film production and their roles. It allows audiences to put a name to faces and remember actors and cast members.

demo reel – A short collection of clips from previous projects that actors have worked on. It demonstrates what talents or skills they would bring to any project.

director – A director gives direction to the cast and crew about acting and the technical aspects to create an overall vision for a film.

ethnically ambiguous – A description for someone whose ethnicity is not easily defined by appearance. An ethnically ambiguous actor can play a role or character of various backgrounds.

executive producer – A producer that is not involved in the technical aspects of the filmmaking process but is still responsible for the overall production. They handle business and legal issues.

extras – An actor in a film who appears in the background, usually in a nonspeaking role.

headshot – A photograph that captures a close shot of an actor's head.

honey wagon – A small trailer that contains one or more dressing rooms, as well as crew bathrooms.

IMDb – An online database of information related to films, television programs, home videos, video games, and streaming content.

improvisation – Acting out a scene with no preplanned script.

mark – A spot, usually marked on the floor or ground with tape or chalk, that shows the exact position(s) given to an actor on a set. This ensures they are in the proper light and camera angle.

monologue – A lengthy, uninterrupted speech given by an actor.

nondisclosure agreement (NDA) – A legally binding contract or confidentiality agreement where an actor agrees not to share any information about a film with a third party.

off book – When an actor has their lines completely memorized.

outside shoot dates – The dates when a film production will be shot (full duration from start to end). An actor may not be required for the full period, but they should be available to go to set if needed during that time.

pilot – A sample of a television show that producers try to sell to networks.

pilot season – A period of time, typically between January and April, when film producers create samples of new shows.

pinned – When an actor is recommended as a potential casting choice to producers. It does not mean an actor has the role, but that they are being seriously considered for it.

premiere – The first public presentation of a film.

principal (role) – A main actor's role that includes lines.

producer – The person responsible for managing the behind-the-scenes aspects of a film production, including the planning, coordinating, managing, editing, marketing, and distribution of a film.

GLOSSARY

script – The written text of a film, including instructions for the actors and for filming.

self-tape – A video of an actor reading and acting for a part that is sent to the casting director for consideration.

set etiquette – The dos and don'ts of working on set. Film production can be complex, and it is extremely important to understand in advance the rules of what is expected of an actor.

sides – Certain pages of a script used for auditions, shooting, etc. The term "sides" is just another word used in the film industry for "script."

slate – When an actor introduces themselves in an audition. The exact information provided depends on what the casting call asks for but usually includes name, height, and location.

stand-ins – Extra actors used as substitutes for featured actors in order to set the lights and rehearse the camera moves.

SWF (starting/working/finishing) – A note on a call sheet that says when an actor is starting, working, and finishing on that day. You may also see SWF in different iterations, such as SW or WF.

table read – When actors and the production team of a film sit down and read a script together aloud for the first time so everyone gets a feel for and can prepare for what it will be like on set.

typecasting – When an actor is constantly cast in similar parts with similar characteristics without variation. It makes it difficult for the actor to find work playing other characters.

V.O. (voice-over) –When an actor does off-camera voices for a film.

wardrobe – The clothing an actor wears on camera while filming.

wrap – When the day's filming is completed, or when the entire production is done.

About the Actor

Olivia Kate Iatridis

Olivia is Inuvialuk, a member of the Inuvialuit Settlement Region in the Western Arctic. She was born and raised in Yellowknife, Northwest Territories. In her teen years, she lived in Alberta, where she began her acting career.

Olivia has played roles in demonstration videos, short and feature films, commercials, and television series, and is a main presenter in a massive open online course on the Arctic offered by the Universities of the Arctic. Most recently, Olivia co-starred in a lead role of the feature film *Abducted*, in which she played Lakota Sampson. Olivia has starred in the ABC

Television Series *Alaska Daily* as Liza Peters. She also played the role of Sadie in the Hallmark film *Sweeter Than Chocolate*.

Olivia has won three Joey Awards (Canada's original and most prestigious awards for young performers): Best Supporting Actress in a Short Film (*Indra's Awakening*), Best Actress in a Commercial (Mattress Mattress), and Outstanding Indigenous Performer.

Olivia is also an avid artist who uses a variety of media to draw and paint.

For more information on Olivia:

Instagram – @oliviakatei

Facebook – Olivia Kate Iatridis

Website – www.oliviakateiatridis.com

About the Author

Gloria Iatridis
Kinnukana

Gloria is Inuvialuk, a member of the Inuvialuit Settlement Region in the Western Arctic. She was born and raised in Tuktoyaktuk, Northwest Territories.

Over her thirty-year career, Gloria has worked in a variety of capacities for the public services sector of the governments of the Northwest Territories, Alberta, and the federal government. Gloria considers her most successful endeavour to be her role as a supportive mother and champion to her children, Olivia and Michael.

Gloria loves being a mother and decided early on that she would nurture and support whatever passions her children had. She believes that any child can do whatever they set their mind to and that parents should be there to support them and guide them to success. Gloria is one of Olivia's greatest fans and will continue to support her throughout her acting career.